TEARS OF
ANGELS
Written by the poet and novelist
Khalil Altahhan

Tears of angels

A Novel

Written by the poet and novelist

Khalil Altahhan

Also by khalil altahhan:

Before you shed my blood

يوميات جرح دمشقي

Te Prophecy of the Eternal Winter.

Tears of angels

I dedicate this novel to the soul of Queen Marie Antoinette, who came to me in a dream in 2006 and inspired me to write this novel and told me that everyone wronged her and I must do justice to her with this book.

introduction:

A novel whose events take place during the French Revolution, a legendary love story between a nobleman and a poor commoner girl.

In the novel, these are real historical figures who lived through that period, such as Marie Antoinette, Louis XVI, and others, they interact with the rest of the novel's characters.

It is the first novel I ever wrote in my life in 2006, and I consider it the closest novel I have ever written to my heart

I hope you like it.

It is the evening hour, casting the elite of melancholy over the dark plains, And pouring upon the paths the cup of bitterness and tears.

There is someone suffering in this moment, so let us listen, friends.

One of the cold nights of December in the year 1799,

In a house in one of the villages overlooking the Seine River on the outskirts of Paris,

a weak woman is dying.

Her age!? She had not yet reached twenty-six, but the signs of life's violence were evident on her clear face and exhausted, collapsed body.

She is Catherine, that was her name.

A name that no longer meant anything to her, for all she could think of was the name of the person who saved her life many times, and ultimately destroyed her life in the end.

She remembers the wasted years, contemplating through a bleak window silent snowflakes, and a wind with a howling voice, among the mist, the image of that old face appears, with its long hairand the nobleman's hat, and the elegant military uniform.

Her mind recalls that moment, the moment of their first meeting.

***

Ten years ago, in the year 1789.

Paris under the rule of Louis XVI, the last king of France, and also under the oppression of clear class discrimination between the ruling nobility and the poor people, or in other words, the commoners, who suffered from poverty, hunger, and homelessness.

And this class, in turn, began to groan from what it was suffering, warning of the beginning of the French Revolution, which would not only change France but also change the world, it will also change the course of Catherine's life.

That little girl who had not yet reached sixteen.

She left her village after her parents died and remained alone with no refuge or shelter, which forced her to go to Paris to seek a living.

While Catherine was sitting in her torn gray dress in one of the streets of Paris not far from the royal Palace of Versailles.

A massive procession advances through the crowd of that street.

Someone shouts: Clear the place quickly, make way for the procession.

Catherine did not move from her place, or rather, she could

not move, as she was engulfed in sorrow, exhaustion, and weakened by hunger, for she had not tasted any food for more than two days.

While she was unconscious in this state, she hears words from a feminine voice: What are you doing here, little girl?

She opened her eyes to the sound of those words, and saw a lady, one of the most beautiful women, wearing a dress embroidered with diamonds and sapphires.

It was Queen Marie Antoinette, who got off her royal carriage, and here she is standing in front of her, with all her beauty, majesty, and brilliance.

Catherine could not believe what her eyes saw,

She could not speak, and before she could try, Queen Antoinette departed and boarded her carriage, and said to one of the guards in a royal voice:

Go and give that poor girl whatever she wants.

That knight approached her, and gave her a bag full of money,

Catherine looked at him and smiled,

He raised his military hat and bowed before her, saying softly: My name is François, what is your name, my dear?

She replied, smiling: I am Catherine.

François extended his hand and held hers, then helped her to stand on her feet, then kissed her hand in the nobleman's manner,

Catherine blushed with embarrassment, and before she could say any word, François left, and after walking a few steps, he turned towards her, saying:

If you need anything, I am at Versailles Palace,

Just tell the guards that you want to meet me, and they will show you where I am,

And he continued on his way until he reached the Queen's procession,

And the procession departed moments later,

Catherine remained stunned for hours, thinking about what happened to her,

While she was lost in her thoughts,

She felt a hand reaching out to her and caressing her face opportunistically,

And then three beggars stood in front of her and began to address her with vulgar and obscene words, and one of them approached her carrying a knife in his hand, saying:

Give me the money you have, little bitch!

Catherine, trembling voice: I have no money, please leave

me alone,

That person's looks at her became more contemptuous and cruel, and he said to her:

I saw you taking money from that vile nobleman!

Catherine felt afraid, and out of fear, she gave them the money, but they did not stop there!

Instead, they attacked her and began to tear her clothes and assault her brutally,

Leaving her lying on the ground, blood flowing from her face and body.

She remained unconscious for hours,

She opened her eyes to the sound of raindrops,

She looked around, the street was empty of passersby.

The rain began to fall more heavily, and the fog filled the place.

The cold began to seep into her body, which had nothing but that torn gray dress,

She tried to get up, but she could not, for her body was too weak to carry her.

The rain became stronger and stronger, the fog increased, and the street became more desolate, except for ghosts. She began to crawl on the ground until she reached a corner of the street to protect her body from the rain, and sat curled up in that corner,

She began to remember her mother, who passed away, and the days of childhood in her village and the green meadows where she used to play with her friends.

The tape of her life passed before her eyes, a tear began to trickle down her cheek,

She was alone now and weak, no one cared for her, noone protected her, and now she faces an unknown fate in a city whose inhabitants have turned into wolves,

Her body began to weaken. She lay on the ground crying until she lost consciousness.

She opened her eyes under the influence of a kiss on her lips and words in a low voice:

Don't be afraid, my dear Catherine, I am François, I willnot harm you.. I will take you to a safe place.

Catherine looked at him and couldn't utter a single word, unable to speak. François carried her in his arms and began to walk under the rain, which was gradually easing, as the first rays of sunlight began to appear.

 It was around half past five in the morning. At that moment, Catherine felt, nestled between François's arms, a tenderness she had never known throughout her miserable life. Perhaps that moment was the first bud of love growing in Catherine's heart!

 Her heart that had turned into a withered flower.

 François carried her until they reached Versailles Palace, then to his room, where he laid her on his bed and began to treat the wounds on her body with his hands and feed her and give her drink.

 Until that moment, Catherine had not spoken a word. She remained dazed by what was happening, and finally, her lips uttered softly to François:

 "Why did you do this to me? Why me?

 I am just a girl from the common people, and you are of noble birth!"

François smiled and said: "Because I...

" and stopped. Catherine asked:

Because what?"

François said: "If I tell you, I fear you will think I am taking advantage of your situation for evil purposes!

Catherine insisted: "Tell me why, and I won't think anything.. You are much better than others anyway, and your actions do not indicate any evil intentions. I have very few choices in this life now, so just tell me."

François smiled, saying: "Your words belie your age!

 It's as if I hear a mature lady speaking! not a teenage girl barely sixteen!

" Catherine replied: "Hardship and homelessness teach a person a lot. Anyway, you haven't answered my question yet!"

François's smile faded, and a look of sadness appeared on his face as he said:

 "Because I...

" Catherine pressed: "Because what?"

 François hesitated and then said: "Because I...

" Before he could finish his sentence, he straightened up, left the room, and walked away.

Catherine smiled as if she had heard him say that word, "Because I love you," wishing it were true.

Tears began to trickle down her cheeks again; she didn't know why she was crying. Perhaps because she had grown accustomed to tears. François watched her from behind the door without her noticing.

He watched her lying on his bed as if she were a forest of flowers, admiring her snow-white face, her blonde hair, and her angelic, almost childlike body, which contained newly blossoming roses.

He continued to gaze at her for a long time until she succumbed to sleep.

He then closed the door and left.

Catherine remained asleep for hours. She woke up to the sound of the door opening.

François entered and sat on the corner of the bed, asking her, "How are you feeling now? Have you improved?" Catherine replied: "Yes, I'm feeling better. Thank you for everything you've done for me."

François said: "No need to thank me; it's my duty.

 Anyway, I was going to tell you... I was just with Queen Marie Antoinette, and I spoke to her about you, told her your story, and how I found you this morning, and begged her to secure a job for you here at Versailles Palace. She agreed and requested that you appear before her as soon as possible."

Catherine said: "Queen Marie Antoinette! I remember her. She is a lady in every sense of the word, and kind to the extreme."

François said: "Then come with me now to appear before her." Catherine got up excitedly to go.

François said: "Slow down, take your time. Is this how you want to meet the queen? In this torn dress? Besides, King

Louis XVI will be present, and he pays close attention to appearances. If he sees you in this dress in the throne room, it will be disastrous."

Catherine asked: "So what's the solution?"

François thought for a moment, opened a wardrobe in his room, and took out a beautiful dress, giving it to her, saying: "This is a dress I have. I sometimes give it to the women who come to me. I hope this doesn't cause you any embarrassment or any problems."

Catherine replied: "It's fine. No problem."

François said: "Then wear it, and I'll wait for you outside.

" When Catherine finished dressing, she left the room like a princess.

François escorted her to the throne room, his eyes never leaving her throughout the journey, as he was amazed by her beauty.

Catherine's cheeks blushed at François's gaze.

François smiled, saying: "I used to think Antoinette was the most beautiful woman in this palace. After meeting you, my conviction has changed somewhat."

Catherine's cheeks blushed even more at his words.

François continued: "Since ancient times, mankind has

dreamed of flying. they always looked at the moon, dreaming of reaching it.

Have you heard of that Arab person who made wings for himself, trying to fly?"

Catherine said: "Yes, I think I've heard of him before. But what reminded you of him now?"

François said: "Your presence with me reminded me of him."

Catherine asked: "What does my presence have to do with it?"

François replied: "He tried to fly. Perhaps that person dreamed of flying to the moon. I once thought of undertaking this adventure myself, but I backed down because I discovered that the moon walks beside me now." Catherine said, a smile tinged with anger on her face: "François, is this flirtation? Are you flirting with me now, I suppose?"

François said:"Yes, didn't you like that flirtation?"

Catherine smiled: "No, that's not what I meant.

But you could have been more direct and said to me, 'You are like the moon,' and spare yourself the trouble of introductions. You always tire me with your confessions."

François said: "Well, well! what do you want me to confess then? Anyway, I have plenty of flirtatious words in my arsenal. Take this one for example:

'The earth's curvature resembles that of a sphere...

'" Catherine interjected: "look at that lady who passed by! looking at me with strange looks! I never liked her looks!"

 François asked: "Do you mean Countess de Barry? who passed by us a while ago?"

Catherine replied: "I don't know her name, and I've never seen her before. Besides, her looks at you were also strange! I wonder why!

 François interrupted: Forget about her for now; her story is long. I'll tell you about it later. Let's return now to our topic we were discussing earlier. Oh, I remembered; we were talking about earth's curvature and...."

Catherine interrupted: "Won't you be quiet, François?" François said: "Yes, my beautiful lady, I won't flirt with you anymore unless you ask me to."

Catherine said, "I won't ask, and you'll do it

By the way, is the throne room far? I'm tired of walking.How big is this palace?"

François replied: "Not very far. It's at the end of the corridor and a little to the left. And did your beautiful feet get tired?"

Catherine retorted, "I didn't ask you!"

Francois: "My apologies, my sweet little one. I forgot. Your beauty always makes me forget my mind.

Catherine: "Where are you trying to reach?"

Francois: "I want to reach your room tonight if you don't mind. But for now, we've reached the throne room. Prepare yourself and don't panic. Be strong and confident in yourself to impress the king and queen. And don't forget to perform the royal greeting, or else you'll be in big trouble.

Catherine Bartabak: Royal greeting?! How! I don't know!

Francois: It's simply a small curtsy, it's not that difficult. Don't worry.

When entered, they saw King Louis XVI sitting on the throne chair with Queen Marie Antoinette, who greetedher with an innocent smile.

From her confusion, Catherine forgot to greet the king and queen! which angered the king, shouting at Francois: "Who is this girl with you?

Doesn't she know how to perform the royal greeting? Doesn't she know how to meet kings? I think she's just a commoner. Her attire won't hide her true self...

Before he could finish, Queen Marie Antoinette got up, ran towards Catherine, took her hands, and said:

"Come with me, let me show you around the palace.

The king shouted, "When will you stop these childish behaviors? Come back here before I act in a manner unfit for a queen.

" But Antoinette ignored him, pulled Catherine by her hand out of the throne room, and began showing her around the palace. Then she took her to her room and invited her to sit.

Catherine was amazed by the queen's spontaneous actions. Despite her spontaneity and humility, she remained the queen in the end.

Antoinette sat beside her and said:

 "It's okay, Catherine. I think your name is Catherinen.. if I remember correctly! Francois told me about you."

Catherine: "Yes, ma'am, that's correct. My name is Catherine."

Antoinette, smiling: "Francois, do you love him?"

Catherine was surprised by the question and said: "Ma'am, you can't ask me that question! I mean, sorry, you can ask me,, but I don't have a clear answer to your question!

Antoinette: "Love cannot hide itself, even if you try to hide it under any mask. Don't evade it. Love is evident in your eyes and clearly visible. Confess, there's no point in denial.

Catherine: "I think so. I love him. But may I ask you, ma'am, if you don't mind, do you love your husband, the king?"

Antoinette, smiling: "And you, young girl! how dare you ask such a question?

Catherine: "Sorry, I overstepped my bounds. Please forgive my intrusion, ma'am."

Antoinette's sadness became apparent on her face. She remained silent for a moment, then answered:

 "If you're asking about my marriage, I married him when I was about your age, almost. All I remember is that my mother, the Empress of Austria, told me that I must marry the grandson of the King of France! namely Louis XVI, who is currently reigning. She said that my marriage would be for the good of the empire. All I remember about my relationship with Louis is that at the beginning of our marriage, he was weak, naive, with a weak personality. He has become very temperamental lately, quick to anger. Honestly, I haven't had a single peaceful day with him. This has been my situation for many years now."

Catherine: "I'm sorry, ma'am, for upsetting you. But have you never experienced love even once in your life?"

Antoinette: "Yes, I have loved. It was a long time ago, almost since I came to France. He was a wonderful young man, much like Francois. I loved him with all my heart, and he loved me too, but fate had other plans for us, and we parted ways.

 Anyway, dear Catherine, I have a suggestion. What do you think about going out with me to stroll in the city?

"Do you believe it? For many years, I haven't left the palace except with the guards! I want to go out, even if just once, to run in the streets of Paris. I want to breathe fresh air. I feel suffocated here in this palace. I'm tired of all this nonsense. I want to be free, even if just for once in my life."

Catherine: "Ma'am, I'd rather you not leave the palace!

Antoinette stood up and pulled Catherine by her hand, saying: "Forget about that talk, let's go out now!

Catherine stopped Antoinette and said in a trembling voice: "No, please, ma'am, don't do it..

Antoinette: "Why not?"

Catherine: "Your presence in the city won't be safe. People outside have turned into wolves, like rabid dogs, ready to devour any noble they see in front of them, especially you. Your outing would be very dangerous..

Antoinette: "But why do they hate me? What have I done to them? And why have people reached the state you describe to me?"

Catherine: "I don't want to burden you with matters that upset you, but I ask you to look around you more deeply to know the truth.

Antoinette didn't understand Catherine's intention. She smiled and said: "Anyway, you will be my lady-in-waiting, and I will prepare a room for you to sleep in here in the palace. And now come with me, and I'll show you to your room.

Catherine went to her room. She lay on her bed. She was very happy, feeling like a princess at this moment. But something inside her told her that this grace would not last long. She did not feel comfortable.

Her thoughts conflicted until she heard knocks on the door. It was Francois. He entered and sat near her bed with a changed expression.

Catherine: "What's wrong? Tell me!

Francois: "Things are changing outside the palace, and the situation is worsening. Poverty among the people has reached an unbearable level, and they have begun to move in an unprecedented and unfavorable way.Despite everything happening, King Louis XVI refuses to negotiate with the common people and refuses to make any concessions to the poor. As for Queen Marie Antoinette, she is drowning in her indifference and extravagance. That's why she's one of the most hated nobles among the common people."

Catherine: "No, Francois, Queen Antoinette is not as bad as

you paint her to be.. I felt her kind heart. She hasa much kinder heart than you can imagine. I also noticed that behind her innocent childish smile, there is a sadness unknown to anyone."

Francois fell silent for a moment, then said:

"I would be lying if I denied my love for her. Of course, my love for her is like that of a subject for his beautiful queen. If anyone tells you they hate Antoinette, they are lying to you or to themselves. If you were to delve into the depths of any French citizen, you would find a great love for the queen. But poverty has blinded their hearts. The poor, who cannot afford their daily bread, cannot love.. when poverty enters the door, love goes out the window..

Catherine, smiling: "Despite my reservations about your words! the poor can also love, perhaps more than the rich! and the person in front of you, talking to you now, is proof of that...

Francois smiled and said: "I don't want to argue with you about who is loved more, me, the rich one, or you, the poor one!

Anyway, the queen's kindness won't change people's attitudes towards the ruling class.. She barely leaves the palace and knows nothing about the suffering of the people outside. The king, for his part, always tries to hide from her what is happening around her. Besides, Antoinette's innocent childish heart and her pampered mind can't even bear the mere thought of someone who doesn't have enough to eat."

My imagination, once i was told her that people were suffering from hunger and didn't even have bread to eat, she innocently replied:

"Then let them eat cake!.. imagine!" ..

 Anyway, she wouldn't be able to do anything, as the commands and prohibitions were in the hands of her husband the king, Louis XVI, who had qualities unfit for a man, and his shaky personality was too weak to command or forbid anything! and if he issued any command, it was either foolishly emotional or hysterically insane. He was also immersed in his pleasures and mistresses, so the kingdom, in my opinion, was on the verge of a major collapse. Despite all the king's flaws, I won't hold him responsible for everything that happens. He inherited a great burden of problems from his grandfather, King Louis XV, which had led France to this disastrous state. Instead of solving these problems, he exacerbated them. Furthermore, financial scandals continued to shake the state, with a new scandal reported every day. People still haven't forgotten the scandal of the diamond necklace from years ago, which greatly tarnished

Queen Marie Antoinette's reputation.

Catherine asked him:

"The scandal of the diamond necklace - I've heard a lot about it since I was young! and rumors abound, but I want to know from you exactly, what is the story of that necklace?"

Francois replied:

"In short, this story happened about four years ago. It happened because of a person named Cardinal Rohan,who claimed that Queen Marie Antoinette wanted to buy a diamond necklace and convinced jewelers in Paris that he was acting as an intermediary between themand the queen. With an agreement between Rohan and his mistress, Countess de La Motte, he took the diamond necklace, claiming he would deliver it to the queen and promised the jewelers to pay for it later. Then the necklace disappeared. The jewelers demanded payment for it, but of course, the queen didn't pay because she didn't receive anything, which angered the jewelers and the public, leading to court proceedings where the cardinal was accused of fraud and sentenced to exile. As for Countess de La Motte, she was whipped and sentenced to life imprisonment but later escaped from prison. Simply put, Rohan wanted to deceive both the queen and the jewelers, exploiting his religious position in the church and the trust the jewelers had in him due to this position. After taking the necklace from the jewelers, he gave it to the countess, who in turn deceived him and took the necklace for herself. Thus, the queen became a victim of a trio of swindlers."

Catherine: "I understand from what you said that the queen is innocent of this matter!! So why was this scandal attributed to her?! And where did the necklace disappear?"

Francois: "Yes, my dear Catherine, the queen is completely innocent. But people talk and assume the worst. They still believe that the queen took the necklace, cheated the jewelers, and didn't pay them. They implicated her by associating her with Cardinal Rohan and thecountess. That's what they think, but the truth is completely different. I heard that the necklace was found in London, and the countess's husband took the necklace there, where it was broken and sold. Anyway, rest assured that the queen is innocent of everything said about her.

In any case, what do you think of taking a stroll around the palace? Don't worry about the situation outside; you can't be afraid when I'm with you.

Francois took Catherine's hand, and they went out together. Catherine spent one of the most beautiful days of her life with Francois, and after this intimate and eventful day, she returned to her room and surrendered to sleep.

In another room of the palace, larger and more luxurious than Catherine's room, this room lacked only a littleto become like the queen's room, a room filled with famous paintings by the most important painters of that era. A woman in her thirties with semi-short curly blond hair sat on a golden rocking chair, holding a fan made of pure gold in her right hand. Of course, the weather wasn't so hot as to require such a fan. She was Countess Julie Anna de Barry.

She hears knocks on the door of her room, signaling one of the maids to open the door.

It's Francois, entering and bowing before her as noblemen usually do..

 Julie looks at him indifferently, then gestures to her maid to leave the room.

Francois holds the maid's hand to prevent her from leaving, then turns to the countess, saying:

"My lady, your attempts with me are no longer useful!Please tell me what you want to say, as I have little time and much to do.

The countess screams at the maid: "I told you to leave, you damned woman, do what I say immediately!"

Before she could finish her sentence, Francois interrupts her: "Excuse me, my lady, but I must leave now.

And he turns to leave.

The countess gets up from her chair and runs towards François, trying to hug him, but he pushes her away, saying:

"I don't want to repeat myself; there's no use in your attempts..

She looked at him angrily and then said: "I sent you a message to come more than two days ago," and now you come to me in this way! François, I love you, so why do you treat me in this cruel way? I have given you everything you want... I made you the most important guard in this palace, and I advised the king to make your salary is greater than the salary of any official in the royal court. I also recommended that the king make you a personal guard for Queen Antoinette, and before you were just an ordinary soldier in the army.. I gave you all of this!

But you didn't give me anything!

François: Madam... I have always been loyal to my work... and in the end I did not ask you for anything... but you know very well that my arrival at this position was not thanks to you... and I think you remember that incident that the Queen was exposed to years ago, and you remember how you saved her from the hands of some common people who wanted to kill her.. you remember that as a result of that story, I reached where I am now, on the recommendation of

Queen Antoinette, who wanted to return the favor to me..

in any case, if you've given me anything, I thank you for it!

I can only thank you for everything you've done.

I want to thank you for everything, for the position, for the high salary, and also for the betrayal!.

Do you remember? or do you want me to remind you? Your memory seems to have weakened these days."

The countess, confused: "Don't you want to forget that story? It was just a passing whim, a fleeting relationship. Do you want to blame me for it for the rest of my life!

Francois, mockingly: "You call it a passing whim and a fleeting relationship?! By God, answer me, woman. Do you consider your presence with three men a passing whim, a fleeting relationship? Do you consider your betrayal to me with three men at once just a passing whim?!! This is not just betrayal; it's clear deviation!

 It's better for you to be silent and never utter a word of love again. I'm not the one who got bitten by the same hole twice. And if you've given me anything, as you claim, don't blame me for what you've given. Otherwise, I'll have to leave the entire palace. and i,ll return as an ordinary soldier. So, I advise you not to trample over my pride, for my dignity is more important than you and all this nobility.

The Countess angrily interrupts: I know why you're preoccupied with me! It's that whore you brought from the street! ..Don't deny it; your story is on everyone's lips.

Francois replies: I won't deny it. Why would you think I would?! This is a personal matter concerning me, and you have no part in it.

The Countess: Is that what you're saying?! When it concerns you, it's a personal matter, and when it concerns me, you call it betrayal!!

Francois: Remember, after your betrayal, I told you plainly that everything between us was over, and everyone was free to act as they pleased. There was nothing between us.. I loved you at some point, or at least tried to, and I was loyal to you beyond measure. As for you...

The Countess interrupts: You disappoint me, and there's no point in discussing it with you. But I'll take an action with that bitch who wants to take you from me. You are mine.

Francois: I swear, if Catherine suffers any harm, I will make you regret it. I advise you to take my words seriously.

Then he left the room.

The Countess de Bari was seized by a fit of madness, and she began to break everything in the room, screaming: "You're mine, Francois, despite yourself."

✳ ✳ ✳

One of the poor streets of Paris at night.

 The street appeared desolate under the influence of intense darkness and the atmosphere of misery and poverty surrounding the houses. The moon looked pale behind dark clouds, emitting a faint ray reflecting on Francois's face as he sat on the steps of a dilapidated house with his friend Roger.

Roger, a handsome young man about thirty, with long hair leaning slightly towards blond, dressed somewhat shabbily, with an old wound on his cheek, turns to him, saying: "Since when have I been telling you to come and work at the palace? I can secure you a decent job there. You're my old friend, and I can't leave you like this."

Roger, with a sad smile on his face, says: "My friend, don't bother convincing me. I swore and won't break my oath. You know that..

Francois: It's a very old story. Haven't all these years passed erased it from your memory?

Roger, after sighing sadly: I loved her, and she denied me. I saved her life, and she killed me. Remember well; we saved her life together, you and I. Why did she repay me with such cruelty?

Francois: I advised you a lot, but you didn't listen to my advice. Man, it's Queen Marie Antoinette, the king's wife and descendant of kings. And you were just an ordinary soldier in the royal court. Moreover, the queen repaid us, you and me, and appointed us to important positions in the army and the palace. But you exceeded your limits with her.

Roger, angrily: And this wound on my face, how can I forget it?!

Francois: You help her, then try to rape her?! And you want her not to defend herself from your despicable actions.

Roger: How dare you!?

Francois interrupts him: Don't get too upset; I didn't mean any harm. You're my friend, and I always want what's best for you. On the other hand, look at me. I respected myself and didn't cross my limits. And here I am, living a happy life. As for you, you were expelled because of what you did.

Roger, angrily: Choose your words carefully. I wasn't expelled; I left the palace with my dignity intact, and I also retired from the army just to preserve my dignity.

Francois: The queen was content with just expelling you despite what you did, and she could have imprisoned you or ordered your death.

Roger, sarcastically and in disbelief: So now I owe her my

life!! Is that what you want to tell me!?

Francois: Antoinette isn't vindictive against you. As you know, her heart is kinder than to hold a grudge. I'm sure she'll forgive you if you apologize to her for your wrongdoing. She might even reinstate you to your job at the palace.

Roger: I won't apologize. I hate apologizing.

Francois: Anyway, you're free to act as you wish.

I want to ask you, is what I heard about you true!?

Roger, playing with a knife in his hand: And what did you hear!?

Francois: I heard that you joined the revolution.

Roger: Who told you that!? And what does it matter to you!? Let's assume what you heard was true. Do you want to arrest me and hand me over to the king!?

Francois: Stop this nonsense. You know I won't do that to a lifelong friend.

Roger: But you'll do it to the other revolutionaries who aren't your friends, right!? Is that what you mean!?

Francois: No, I won't do that either. You know how sympathetic I am to the revolutionaries. I believe the French people deserve a better life.

Roger: Then what compels you to serve those who oppress this people!?

Francois: These are matters and reasons I prefer to keep to myself.

Roger: Ah, I think I understand you now.

✳✳✳

Sunday night, in the banquet hall of the palace, where a masquerade ball was held, as usual, the aristocratic class of nobles was invited.

Catherine is talking to one of the maids of honor.

The maid, Christine: So that's what happened to you. Your story is tragic.

Catherine: Anyway, my situation has improved, as you can see. I have nothing but to thank the Lord for this blessing.

Christine interrupts: Catherine, look at that lady standing there with the king. Haven't you seen her?! That arrogant lady!

Catherine: Yes, I saw her. What about her?

Christine: She's Madame Julie Anne de Barry, the wife of Count Alain Boissey, who died about three years ago.

Catherine: What's it to me?

Christine: Her close confidante told me that she intends harm for you. So be careful and don't get involved in any trouble with her.

Catherine: But why does she want to harm me?! And why does she hate me?!

Christine: She loves Francois. I think you understand now what I mean.

Catherine: Does he reciprocate her feelings?!

Christine smiles: You know better, my dear Catherine.

Catherine, embarrassed: Damn you, Christine, won't you stop this teasing and insinuation?!

Christine: Do you love him?!

Catherine, blushing: Shut up, you cursed one!

Christine: Pay attention, Catherine. She keeps staring at you repeatedly. Don't you notice that!! Look, King Louis XVI is also staring at you. You're such a lucky woman.

Catherine: Will you not stop bothering me, you cursed one?

Christine: Look at that handsome young man entering the hall now. He's disguised elegantly.

Catherine: It's Francois.

Christine: I recognized him immediately. Can the moon be hidden? Look, Countess de Barry almost devours him with her eyes. Watch closely. He's ignoring her and heading towards us.

Francois approaches Catherine and kisses her hand, saying, "Would you allow me this dance?"

Catherine: But I don't know how to dance.

Francois: You will learn. Just come with me.

François takes her hand and they start dancing.

Catherine feels her body moving effortlessly as if she were a professional dancer of high caliber. Jealousy begins to gnaw at Countess de Barry's heart as she watches this scene. Without realizing what she's doing, she rushes towards them through the crowd, grabs Catherine by her hair, and spits on her face, right in front of Francois. Francois becomes enraged and slaps the Countess across her face, causing her to fall to the ground. The whole hall quiets down under the influence of this scene. The Countess gets up from the ground, screaming and crying.

I, François, am slapped in this manner! how dare you?! insulting me in front of this whore maid and all this large crowd? You will pay dearly for this act!

François mockingly replies: "I won't regret it."

He then grabs Catherine by the hand, leaving the hall. Outside, Catherine appears displeased with everything that happened. She turns to François saying:

"Don't you think you overreacted towards her?"

François responds: "Is that what you think? I did what I did for you! I can't see you being humiliated in front of me like that and stay silent. Besides, she deserves more than that."

Catherine replies: "Regardless of what she did to me, as I heard, she loves you. And those who love do more than this to keep their beloved!

François: you say she loves me!!

I swear you know nothing.

" Anyway, come with me to my room. I have a lot to say, and you must listen to me, my sweet little one.

✳ ✳ ✳

In the king's room after midnight, Queen Antoinette in night clothes, the king enters drunk and heavy-bodied. He looks at Antoinette mockingly, saying in a heavy voice, "Good evening, Queen.

" He throws himself on the bed, then continues in the same heavy voice: "Don't you want to welcome your dear husband?"

Then he laughs foolishly and says: "Am I not the king? As the king, I order you to welcome me now and immediately.

" Antoinette remains silent, not uttering a word.

he grabs her hand and pulls her towards him, saying: "Come closer to me. I want to kiss you.

" Antoinette forcefully pulls her hand away and screams in his face, saying: "Keep your damn lips away from me. And now you want to convince me that you've become a man? Do you want to prove to me your manhood and masculinity? Do you remember or do you want me to remind you?!"

 he angrily rises after Antoinette's words sober him up: "Damn you, bitch. Do you want me to remind you of your cheating on me? Do you remember or do you only remember what pleases you?

Antoinette, screaming: When you become a real man, then you can talk about betrayal. Certainly, manhood, in my opinion, is not the meaning understood by people like you. Manhood is in noble ethics, and you lack manhood in both senses. Even if you possess a small part of the ethical meaning of manhood, I would overlook the first meaning that you and your likes of dirty pseudo-men understand.

The king angrily: Shut up, corrupt one. I am a man despite you and everyone else. I want you to know something important, your time of control over me has passed. Understand this well.

Antoinette: You say I controlled you! You admit with your own tongue that you are not a man! Let's assume I did control you, tell me by the heavens!! What makes a woman control her husband except if he is weak of character? You were the one forcing me to do that. And now you think yourself to be strong of character. Do you want me to tell you what you were and how you've become? You were weak, and you are now weak and filthy. That's the only change that has occurred to you, and it's a truth you cannot deny, neither you nor anyone else.

he bursts into anger and grabs a glass vessel and throws it, nearly hitting Antoinette's head. She stands and says to him: "You are vile. Your heroics only show on women. How vile you are. I mourn for a country whose leader is you. I swear you will lead us all to an abyss." Antoinette leaves the room, looking at the king with disdainful glances.

A corner of one of the poor streets of Paris.

Roger walks nervously back and forth in his place, surrounded by about twenty people from the public.

One of them says: "How long will we wait? How long will we remain satisfied with some simple actions here and there?"

Another says: "We must expand our operations further and

strike more strongly.

" Roger replies: "They've uncovered our weapon caches and seized a large part of them, but don't worry. A large quantity of weapons will come to us from some friends who smuggled them from Britain by sea. It's just a matter of time, and those weapons will reach us.

However, their arrival requires great caution, as soldiers are scattered around Paris, and smuggling them is somewhat difficult. And when the weapons arrive, rest assured we will move to the next big step.

" Someone asks: "And what is this step?

Roger: The storming of the Bastille. We will raid it. This is the step we planned and all the leaders of the revolution agreed on. I know it's a difficult step, but we will achieve it if we cooperate.

" Someone says: "I heard that Queen Antoinette's procession will pass through the neighboring street tomorrow morning. I was thinking that..

" Roger interrupts him: I swear to God, whoever harms her in any way, his end will be at my hands first.

" The voices of those present rise: "But she is our enemy!.

" Roger angrily: I think you heard my words, and there's no need for me to repeat them. Whoever thinks of harming

Antoinette should know that he will face me first. The debate ends.

✳✳✳

The next day, the queen's procession...

Today, the weather is unstable. It seems it's going to rain.

The attendant: My lady, you're right. We should quickly reach the palace.

Antoinette, smiling as she looks out of the carriage window: Look at that person. He's a flower vendor.

She orders the carriage to stop and tells the attendant, "He has beautiful flowers. I'll go and buy some."

The attendant: But, my lady...

Antoinette gets out of the royal carriage and rushes towards the vendor, starting to pick flowers.

She hears footsteps around her, turns with fear, and sees about seven people. Then more approach from the narrow alleys between the houses.

One of them says, "So, you're the arrogant queen!

Then, he turns to another, asking: What should we do with her? Should we take her captive to negotiate with the king for our demands? or should we kill her and rid this land of her arrogance? Or perhaps..."

At that moment, those people disperse as a gunshot is heard from behind them!

It's Roger, steadily approaching, making his way through the crowd who start to move aside for him. He stands in front of them, saying:

"Didn't you understand what I told you yesterday?"

One shouts, "You're defying the laws of the revolution!

Roger, smiling mockingly, fires at one of them, killing him. He continues: "Tell me, what laws!? This is the law of the jungle. The strong eat the weak!

Whoever among you wants to try this law and meet the fate of your friend, then come closer to the queen..

Everyone starts to retreat.

Roger's gaze hardens, and he fires another shot, hitting another person, who falls dead.

The others flee in terror.

He then turns his back and leaves without even looking at Antoinette, who dropped the flowers from her hand, stunned by the scene she witnessed.

She continued in a daze until she reached her royal carriage.

* * *

In Queen's chamber, in the evening...

Francois enters and bows, greeting, "I was worried about you, my lady. I heard about what happened to you today."

Antoinette: It was Roger.

Francois: What!? Did he harm you again?

Antoinette: No, he saved me from some people who tried to kill me.

Francois, smiling: I'm sorry, my lady, but I'm not surprised by his behavior. He still loves you.

Antoinette: But I'm afraid of him. He was and still is frightening with his actions.

Francois: You're right. But his heart is kind beyond measure.

Antoinette: True, Francois.

"Tell me, where has he been all this time after leaving the palace?"

Francois: His story is long. He went to America and participated in the American Revolution against the British occupation. He inflicted heavy losses on the English. He was known for his brutality, killing English soldiers in very harsh ways without any mercy. Some there called him the monster, and others called him the Revolution's Terror. Anyway, he was eventually captured, taken to Britain, and imprisoned there for a while. But he incited the prisoners who revolted inside the prison and escaped after committing a massacre in which more than fifty English soldiers were killed. He returned to France and joined the revolution. That's all..

Antoinette: What a bloody history! And you want me not to fear such a man!?

Francois, smiling: But his heart is kind.

Antoinette: You say his heart is kind! Get out of my face then..

Francois smiles and bows, saying:

"Yes, his heart is kind, and time will prove my words to you.

"Now, please allow me to leave," and he leaves the room.

✳✳✳

In one of the palace corridors...

The attendant Christine talks to another attendant, Laura.

Christine: I saw them with my own eyes.

Laura: Do you mean Francois? Tell me, what else did you see?

Christine: I saw more than you can imagine. He entered her room and...!

Look, look! Do you see what I see!?

Laura: Is that Countess Debari!?

But why is she so upset and angry!?

Christine: She's heading to Catherine's room!

Laura: I don't know why she's so upset, but I'm sure she's bringing trouble with her.

Christine: The countess's temperament is very difficult. May God help Catherine. I think tonight won't end well.

Laura: Tell me the story. Do you know something I don't?

Christine: I'll tell you.. The story is that Catherine came to the palace, and...

✳ ✳ ✳

In Catherine's room...

Countess Debari enters without permission, approaching Catherine and brandishing a knife towards her face.

Then she says, "Do you know, you wretch, I can now disfigure your beautiful face, or I can kill you outright and throw your body to the dogs."

"Do you know what prevents me from doing that?"

She pauses for a moment. Tears start to well up in her eyes.

Then she repeated her words:

"Do you know why?"

Then she fell to the ground, crying.

Catherine approached her with fear, saying:

"What's wrong, madam?! Are you alright?!"

The Countess raised her head, saying:

"Because I was once like you, one day!

Catherine, surprised: "You were like me!! How?!"

The Countess: "I don't know who my father is, or even my mother. I spent my childhood in an orphanage.

When I left the orphanage, I was your age.

I found myself in a dirty world that only recognizes materialism and money. I didn't meet anyone from the common people without them exploiting me and taking advantage of my weakness.. And when I entered the palace as a maid, I didn't meet anyone from the nobility without them exploiting my weakness. Until I met Count Alan, who asked me to marry him. Of course, I never loved him for a day."

But I had no other choice, so I married him. He seemed better than others, but his behavior changed after a few days of our marriage, as always with men, they start off kind then turn into wild dogs. Why? I don't know!

He began hitting me morning and night, never missing an opportunity to humiliate me.

But I endured, yes, I endured....

she remained silent for a moment, then continued:

"I killed him with these two hands...

Catherine: "You killed him?!

" Countess: "Yes, I killed him. I couldn't bear his humiliation towards me. I pushed him with these hands from the top of the stairs. Everyone thought it was just an accident. I inherited all his wealth, and now I'm one of the richest in the kingdom.

Catherine: "Don't you think by confessing this, you're handing me your murder?"

Countess: "I don't know. All my life I've called myself stupid, but this time, I say what I say with complete comfort. I don't know. When I came to you, I was filled with resentment and hatred. I intended to disfigure or kill you, but suddenly my feelings changed. How did this transformation happen? I don't know. Perhaps because you're like me and your suffering resembles mine, even though you're my rival who took away the only person I truly loved."

Catherine: "But forgive me, madam, for this question. If you loved him, why did you cheated on him?

Countess: "I cheated on him for him...

Catherine in surprise: "You cheated on him for him?!"
Countess: "Yes, you have every right to be surprised! but let me explain so your surprise fades away.

Do you know that François doesn't know who his father is! but I do.. I also know who his father is..

Catherine in surprise: "What?! I mean, how?!"

Countess: "All François knows about his family and lineage is that he's the son of a soldier in the French army whom his mother married after coming to France.

In reality, he's the son of Lord Richard, one of the English army's commanders during the reign of Louis XV.

Do you know who Lord Richard is? I guess you don't..

He's the old enemy of the royal family. He insulted the former King Louis XV during his visit to Britain, and since then, killing him has been an obsession for the former king and his grandson, the current King Louis XVI."

Catherine: "But what does this have to do with the issue of betrayal?"

Countess: "It has everything to do with it.

About two years ago, three men came to me, knowing well how attached I am to François. They claimed to know everything about François's lineage and possessed documents confirming it. They demanded a large sum of money to keep quiet and not present those documents to the king. If the king knew François's lineage, he and his family would have been killed long ago. So, I gave them the money they wanted, but they weren't satisfied. They blackmailed me with other things, and my body was part of these blackmails! I gave it to them only to save François's life!.. François entered the room while we were in a suspicious situation on a day I'll never forget.

He humiliated me in front of them and everyone.

He's not at fault.. he doesn't know, and I didn't tell him to protect his feelings..

Now I have two choices, both bitter, either tell him the truth and hurt his feelings to clear myself in front of him and everyone who accuses me of betrayal, or hide my sacrifice for him, his reputation, and his life, and lose my reputation and his love. But I chose the second option, the sacrifice..

She began to cry bitterly and said:

"But he exaggerates in humiliating me. His insults are unbearable.. and his contempt is intolerable.

" She finished her words and ran out of the room.

∗∗∗

Catherine's room, after midnight She felt the door of her room opening.

She turned her face in fear to know who it was!

it was King Louis XVI. He began to approach her with heavy steps, signs of drunkenness evident on his face.

He sat close to her.

He started getting closer and closer to her.

Catherine begged him to stay away from her.

Then he attacked her violently and disgustingly..

At that moment, François entered the room and pulled the king away from Catherine, saying:

"Please, sir, don't do this. This girl belongs to me. I have several maids, choose from them what you want, but please, leave this girl to me.

The king replied with anger on his face:

"How dare you stop me from a girl I want? And who is this whore to be of such importance to you?

Then he attacked her again in front of François! So, he pulled him away and put his arms around his neck almost choking him, saying:

"Please, sir, don't push me to behave with you in a way you may not forget for the rest of your life.. So, please leave the room now and immediately.

Louis XVI left the room screaming:

"You will regret your actions, François. I promise you'll regret.

François approached Catherine, who was completely shattered, and began to stroke her hair and whisper in her ear,

"Don't worry, my love Catherine, I'm with you now, and I promise I won't let anyone hurt you as long as I'm alive..

He kissed her forehead, and Catherine rested her head on his chest and began to cry..

François comforted her and stroked her hair until she fell asleep.

He stayed by her side all night, and when the sun rose, and he was sure she would be okay, he kissed her forehead and left the room.

One of the poor neighborhoods of Paris..

An old house with a worn-out wooden door that time has

eaten away at, and above that house, an old chimney. Next to that chimney sits a young child not older than ten years old, looking like a chimney sweep. He is called by Roger who was coming from afar:

"Hey, you there! What are you doing up there!?

That's you, John! Come down from there immediately before I come and throw you down from above."

The child John replies: "Sir, I have cleaned the chimney for you..

Roger climbs the house and grabs John by his ear, saying: "You little trickster, so you've cleaned the chimney, huh?"

He laughs and continues: "And now you want me to pay you for it!

Roger searches his pockets but finds nothing but a piece of bread he found in his shirt pocket. He hands it to the child John, saying: "Take this and eat it all."

The child John takes the piece of bread and starts eating it eagerly as if he hadn't tasted food for days.

Roger addresses him smiling: "But don't clean this chimney unless I ask you to. Anyway, I haven't used this fireplace all winter because I have neither firewood nor fuel for heating."

Roger jumps off the roof then heads towards the door. He enters and closes that old door behind him.

Inside, an old woman sits at a round wooden table with a moderately beautiful girl who looks like she's over thirty.

Roger, smiling: "What's wrong with you two?

You seem so down as if a disaster has struck you!

Then he approaches the old woman and kisses her on the forehead, saying:

"What's bothering the beautiful lady Liliurissa?

 What's wrong?"

The girl interrupts him: "Leave your grandmother alone, her worries are enough for her.

Talk to me instead. Tell me where you've been all this time? Don't you know you have relatives we should ask about?! Or do you want us to suffer like your mother and siblings, or have you forgotten!?"

Roger falls into silence, his face showing signs of sadness.

Grandmother Liliurissa: "How many times do I have to tell you, Claudia, leave Roger alone and don't talk to him like that. We want him to forget the pains of the past, and you keep reminding him!?"

Claudia: "We haven't tasted any food for two days, and Roger hasn't even asked if we're alive or dead! Is this fair!?"

Roger, standing upright: "No, my dear niece, it's not like

Roger to forget his family or abandon them.. and now I'll go and get some food and firewood for heating.

Grandmother Liliurissa: "And do you have money to buy what you said!?

Roger: "Don't worry, I'll figure it out."

And he walks away from the place..

Claudia, addressing the grandmother: "Roger doesn't love me. He doesn't care about me at all."

Grandmother: "Don't ever say that. You're his niece, and he won't abandon you."

Claudia sighs and says: "How long will we endure this miserable situation? Poverty is killing us. I can't bear it anymore..

She pauses for a moment then continues: "We must leave for Italy, and we must convince Roger to leave with us because all our cousins are there.

At least we'll live a better life than this life of humiliation here."

Grandmother: "Don't worry, my dear, we'll leave, but at the right time."

After hours when darkness fell,

Roger enters the house carrying some bread and a bundle of firewood.

Grandmother Liliurissa and Claudia were secluded in one corner of the house, and Claudia was trembling, holding a knife in her hand, with signs of horror evident on her face and on the grandmother's face.

Roger, surprised: "What's wrong with you two? Why are you like this!?"

Claudia, trembling: "It's the cellar; something strange is happening down there."

Roger, astonished: "Which cellar are you talking about, you crazy woman!?"

Claudia: "While I was moving the wardrobe in the adjacent room a while ago, I discovered a cellar directly beneath it. And when I tried to open its door, I felt something moving and heard a strange sound."

Roger, laughing: "A cellar! And strange sounds!! What nonsense is this!?"

Grandmother: "Believe her, I heard the sounds too!"

Roger, smiling: "I'll go and investigate, but I hope whatever it is down there is human or even a predatory animal so I can deal with it. But if it's non-human or even supernatural, then

I have a different story with it."

And he laughs, heading towards the cellar..

He opens the door and finds stairs leading downwards into the pitch-black darkness.

He calls out: "Whoever is inside, if you're a man, come out and face me..

No one responds.

Roger continues: "Alright, if you don't want to come out, you'll force me to come down to you..

He descends the stairs and comes out after a few minutes.

He approaches Claudia and the grandmother, laughing, saying: "I liked that cellar. It will be useful for some matters..

Claudia: "Is there anything there?"

Roger: "Will you stop this bullshit? I told you there's nothing there. And even if there was something, as you claim! it won't show up now. Trust me on that..

Claudia screams: "I want to leave this cursed house. Since we moved in, we haven't had a single happy day.

Roger: "You want to leave!? And where will you sleep!? In the street!!? Yes, I bought this old house with all my money, and this is all I have. And if you don't like the house, then go and buy a palace in Versailles with your own money and live in it." (He says it mockingly.)

Claudia: "Then let's go to Italy, as you know we have relatives there..

Roger: "I will never leave France again..

This is my final decision.

✳ ✳ ✳

After a few days..

Catherine is sleeping in her room.

She opened her eyes to the sound of François' footsteps,

She turned towards him and saw him broken,

Before he reached her bed, he fell to his knees, tears filling his eyes.

Catherine got up from her bed, ran towards him.

François lifted his eyes and looked at her with deep sadness, saying:

"This morning, I entered my house outside the palace... then... and tears began to fill his cheeks!

Catherine, anxiously: "Then what? tell me!

He continued, saying: "Then I found my mother and my three sisters murdered and a message thrown beside my mother's head saying: 'This is my first revenge, wait for worse from me!

He paused for a moment, then continued,

He is the cursed king, that immoral libertine, I am sure of that..

And above all this, he has ordered me to be transferred to the French fleet in the Channel, instead of solving his internal problems, he thinks of fighting the English and opening an external front!

But from now on, I will not take orders from anyone..

I will not obey the killer of my mother and sisters, and I swear I will avenge that vile scoundrel..

Catherine hugged him and whispered in his ear:

"I don't know what to say to you, and how to console you! your pain is very severe and I don't know which of our wounds is deeper, yours or mine! and which of our pains is greater, yours or mine!"

But I will tell you, consider me as your lost family members..

When François heard Catherine's words, he threw himself on her chest crying like a little child, tears also fell from Catherine's eyes,,

They hugged each other for a long time, crying until their

tears mixed with each other's, and their sorrow with each other's..

This miserable embrace continued until François raised his head after his tears dried up,

He stood up screaming:

"Now I know what I will do, and I know my path well."

Catherine, with fear: "What do you intend to do?!

He replied, saying: "I will leave the palace and join the crowds..

I will join the revolution,,

And I will not rest, and I will not close my eyes until I see the head of the scoundrel Louis XVI under my feet."

François hurried his steps out of the room. And before he closed the door,

Catherine shouted: "But what about Queen Marie Antoinette?!"

That woman whom you have always loved and defended!

Tell me what about her? and will you be against her too?!

Will your revenge include her as well?!"

François fell silent for a moment, then turned to her saying: "I don't know."

And he turned his face away, leaving,

Catherine shouted again, crying:

"But what about me?!

Are you going to leave me alone here to face my dark fate?!

Are you going to abandon me?!"

He turned to her again and said: "I don't know."

And before closing the door,

Catherine shouted at him: "What about your child in my womb?!"

When François heard Catherine's words, he froze in place, her question struck him like lightning, he entered a state of shock from the horror of the question!

he fell into silence from the shock, and after he recovered from the surprise, he turned to her saying:

After I lost all my family members because of you, I will never pay attention to just a little child.

In any case, it doesn't matter to me anymore, my revenge is greater..

He was silent for a while, then said:

Who said that the child in your womb is my son? He may be someone else's son!

He said this phrase in confusion, his eyes were trembling and his hands were shaking..

and closes the door behind him and left the room,

Catherine could not comprehend what she had heard, she could not believe what she had heard, and she did not want to believe. François, the man she loved with all her heart, was abandoning her so easily, in such a strange way, and in such a tragic manner.

After several days passed,

While Catherine was in one of the palace corridors,

She hears screams from not far away,

She searches for the source of this scream, it's from the Countess de Barry's room!

Catherine runs towards the door of the room, she hears a familiar voice!

It's François's voice that rose in that moment of screaming,

She knocks on the door several times, no one answers, she opens the door and enters,

Countess Julie was sitting on the floor of the room in one corner trembling and crying, and François was standing in front of her with signs of anger on his face!

When Catherine entered, François ordered her to leave..

Catherine refuses, he ignores her and turns to the Countess saying:

"Your baseness will never end, you dirty one, all of you are lowlifes, all of you are scum, you and the king, all of you resemble each other."

Catherine: "François, please stop..

François: "Catherine, don't interfere, don't stick your nose in."

And he continues addressing the Countess:

"Do you want to convince me that you are innocent, that you are a pure human being!"

The Countess, with a trembling voice:

"François, I love you, why don't you want to believe me! How can you think that I can hurt you!?"

François: "If it's not the king, then it's definitely you!

I know you wanted to revenge on me because I slapped and humiliated you in front of everyone..

And he grabs the Countess who was trembling from her hair and pulls her from the ground almost choking her, saying:
"Admit that you are the murderer, you are as vile as the king,

both of you hate me and want to revenge against me,"

Catherine couldn't bear this scene,

She ran towards François and pulled him with all her strength..

François turned towards Catherine saying:

"You, Catherine!! Are you defending her?! Have you forgotten what she did to you?! Have you forgotten how she spat in your face and insulted you?!"

He paused for a moment, then stepped back, and continued:

"Now I understand everything, and the picture has become clear to me!

All of you are in agreement with each other, all of you are in agreement against me, all of you are criminals..

Catherine interrupted him: "You're crazy, François. I swear you've gone mad.

The words you're saying don't come from a sane person. We all understand the difficult situation you're going through, and we appreciate the extent of the tragedy you've experienced with the loss of your mother and sisters. But that doesn't mean you can hurl accusations right and left and accuse people in a mad manner.

Who are you accusing?! You're accusing the people who

loved you?!

François, sarcastically: "You mean the people who loved me?!" Who do you mean by the devil's sake?!

Do you mean this whore - pointing to the countess - this prostitute who loves no one but herself?!"

Catherine angrily: "Damn you, François! The one you describe as a whore and a prostitute is cleaner than you, and purer than you.

If it weren't for her, the worms of the grave would be gnawing your bones now..

If it weren't for her, you would be a lifeless corpse long ago. She sacrificed her money and reputation for you.

You must learn the truth now. Do you know the truth of your lineage?! Do you know who you are the son of?!"

The countess interrupted her, crying: "Please, Catherine, don't tell him."

Catherine screamed: "Are you still defending him?!

Are you still hoping for good from him?

I will speak even if it costs me my life.

" Then she turned to François and said: "You are the son of Richard the Englishman, and you know well who he is and how much the king hates him.

You know that if the king knew you were his son, he would kill you immediately. The men you think the countess betrayed you with knew the truth of your lineage. And this woman you insult and belittle sacrificed her money and gave them her pure body just to silence them and keep harm away from you. She didn't tell you all this time just so as not to hurt your feelings because she loves you..

Now you know the truth.. What do you want now?!"

François fell into moments of silence, then burst into a mocking laugh, saying:

"This is the silliest joke I've ever heard in my life! and you want me to believe this empty talk and be convinced by this nonsense?"

He laughed again, more scornfully, and turned his back to leave the room.

The countess got up from her place and ran towards François, grabbing him by his shirt until she clung to him, saying: "I love you, François. Please don't wrong me.

" He said to her: "Get away from me, cursed one.

" She returned and clung to him, repeating her words.

He pushed her hard, and she fell, hitting her head on the wall. She fell to the ground, blood flowing heavily from her head. Catherine ran towards her, screaming.

The countess began to repeat these words:

"I love you, François, I love you."

These were her last words, and she closed her eyes, leaving life.

Catherine began to scream and cry at the horror of this scene.

François was completely stunned, motionless, because of what his hands had done..

Catherine got up from her place and attacked François, grabbing him by his shirt and started hitting him on his chest and face, screaming: "You killed her, you vile one, damn you! You killed her." François's lips uttered no words. He took Catherine's words and slaps as if something inside him was telling him that he deserved these slaps, even more than that.

He pushed Catherine away from him in desperation and left the room, completely stunned.

Catherine continued to cry by the countess's body for hours.

The case of the countess's murder was brought to court. Catherine was initially accused due to her known hostility towards the countess. But what saved her from the accusation was the testimony of the maid Christine, who overheard the entire conversation inside the room as she passed by there by chance. Her testimony was corroborated by another maid who saw François entering the countess's room before the incident. Thus, François was convicted of the crime. Of course, Louis XVI supported this conviction due to the animosity between him and François. It was the best way to get rid of him. He was sentenced to death in absentia. But of course, the punishment was not carried out, as François was then part of the revolution, and his pursuit was like pursuing all the revolutionaries. Therefore, executing the sentence was almost impossible.

An old room on the outskirts of Paris.

Laurent, one of the leaders of the revolution, is talking to someone who appears to be English, General Robert.

Laurent: "So, you're telling me that the weapons have arrived. Anyway, we thank you for your efforts, and we will reward you for this deed."

Robert: "No need for thanks, we both have an interest in what's happening."

Roger enters with François..

Laurent to Robert: "Let me introduce Roger and François, they are two of the strongest men we rely on.

General Robert to Roger: "So you're the one who killed our soldiers and committed atrocities against them?"

Then he turns to François, smiling a contemptuous smile, saying: "And you, you're the son of the maid..

François: "Excuse me, what did you say!?"

Robert: "You're the son of the maid Theodora, who was raped by General Richard, and you were the result of that rape." He let out a mocking laugh..

François became angry and drew his sword from its sheath, placing it on Robert's neck, and almost killed him if it weren't for the intervention of Commander Laurent, who held him back and calmed him down a little.

He then begged him to leave the room with him.

After they left, General Robert was left alone with Roger, who was standing with his back turned.

Robert to Roger, with fear: "And you, won't you go to your friend?"

Roger turned to him after spitting out a stick he was fiddling with between his teeth for a while, remained silent for a moment.. then threw him with a knife that passed along his face, on which a long line of blood appeared.

And he laughed, saying: "Sorry, a little mistake happened. I meant to hit your eye, but the knife deviated a little.

But don't worry, I'll make it up to you soon."

And he approached him and grabbed him by the neck with his strong hand until Robert's face turned blue, almost choking him. Then he said to him: "No one insults my friends. Do you understand, you dirty Englishman?" Robert, in a choked pale voice: "But what about you? Why did you react like this to me?"

Roger let out a wide laugh and said: "You know what my problem is today? My problem is that today I'm not in the mood to kill. And if I were, your head would have been severed from your body long ago, without any reason. You know me well. I don't need any justification to kill.

" And Roger released his neck, causing Robert to fall to the ground almost unconscious, then he gathered his strength and got back up and sat down.

Roger turned to left the room.

Before closing the door, he turned to Robert and said:

I was going to tell you... Fuck you. You made me forget what I was going to tell you!

He takes a few steps forward, then turns around and says: Ah, "I remembered."

He pulls out another knife he had with him and throws it, piercing Robert's forehead and taking the tip out of the back of his head...

Then he smiles and closes the door, leaves the room.

As he was leaving,

Commander Laurent asked him: "Your voice was raised inside! what happened between you and him?"

Roger smiled, saying:

We used to understand each other on some friendly terms.. that's all that happened. Anyway, go to him and you'll see.

He laughs broadly and continues walking away.

Moments later, Commander Laurent rushes to Roger, saying: "Do you know what you've done? Your actions will cause us many problems. It's a disaster!"

Roger smiles, saying: "Nothing will happen," and continues walking away.

Elsewhere, not far away, Francois sits on a stone beside an old house, his hands covering his face, tears evident on his hands.

Roger approaches him, grabbing his arm, saying:

"Come on, man! I don't like seeing my lifelong friend like this! And what are these tears? It's shameful for men to cry.

"Francois, lifting his head: "My friend, I no longer know anything. I've lost everything. I'm desperate with this life. I've lost my family, my life, everyone who loved me and whom I loved. I see them falling one after another, dying. Those candles that once lit up my life are now extinguishing. I live for nothing now. My life has no meaning anymore, even my dignity is lost.

"Roger smiles: "Take it easy, my friend, I've restored your reputation.

"Francois, with anger in his eyes: "That English scoundrel, I swear I'll be his killer.

Roger: "I spared you the trouble of killing him.

Francois: "What are you saying!? How!?

Roger laughs broadly: "I sent him to hell. I killed him. Actually, from the beginning, I wanted to kill him. You know me well.. I have a hobby I've loved since childhood, the hobby of killing. But don't misunderstand me.. I only kill villains, and I enjoy killing them. It's a pleasure beyond pleasure to cut the throat of a villain or gouge out his eyes. I'm a savage. That's what you're saying about me now!

Francois seems absent, as if he hasn't heard a word from Roger's words.

Roger turns to him: "What's wrong with you? Your mind is not with me. What's with you!?

Francois sadly: "I've lost her forever..

Roger: "Do you mean the girl you told me about? What was her name?

Francois: "And I unjustly treated the second one too!..

Roger: "The second one!! I didn't know about this. Who do you mean!?

Francois: "And I killed her too.

"And he covers his face with his hands to hide tears starting to flow from his eyes.

Roger pats Francois's shoulder: "Stop crying like a woman. It doesn't suit you.

Francois: "Leave me, Roger. You haven't lost like I have, and you haven't lost loved ones like I have!

Roger, his smile fading: "You're wrong, i've lost, and he walks away.

✳✳✳

Roger's house a few days later..

Roger opens the door and enters. He finds a letter on the table near the door.

He opens the letter and reads it. When he finishes reading the letter, signs of anger appear on his face and he says: "So

you did it, Claudia, and went to Italy with my grandmother."
He is silent for a while, then he folds the letter in his hands
and throws it away.

He continues: "In any case, you have relieved me of the
worry of taking care of you."

He says it and opens the door and leaves.

He called a child John, who was cleaning the chimney in a
neighboring house.

He asks him: Where do you and your family sleep these
days?

John: We are sleeping in the adjacent yard under the old
bridge..

Roger: From now on, this house will be yours and your
family's.

You will live and live here permanently..

John: But what about you, sir! Where will you sleep!?

Roger, smiling: "I will take care of myself, so don't worry
about it." And he walks away leaving, saying to himself: "I'm
free now, and I'll draw my own end.

"In Commander Laurent's room, with General Alfred..

Laurent: "I don't know how to apologize to you for what
happened.. but I promise you I'll punish the murderer. Now,

the important thing is the weapons.. This revolution must succeed.

Alfred: "That's what we hope for, that the murderer be punished, and this revolution succeed.. This is useful talk, beneficial for us and for you.

Laurent: "Be confident that Roger will receive the punishment he deserves.. Don't worry.

General Alfred rises from his seat, horror on his face:

"Do you mean Roger Dubier?

Laurent: "Sit down, what's wrong with you!? Do you know him?

Alfred, after calming himself a little: "Forget it,"

and he ends his conversation with Commander Laurent and leaves the room.

As soon as he closes the door and walks a few steps, he sees a person with a huge body standing in front of him. He lifts his head and sees Roger's face, then recoils, trembling.

Roger: "So, you're General Alfred. I see you're alive! you haven't died yet!!

Alfred, with fear: "Stay away from me, what do you want from me?"

Roger turned his back, and signs of anger began to show on

his face: "Anyway, if you didn't die yesterday, you will die today. And if you don't die today, you will die tomorrow. The important thing is that you will die sooner or later. I promise you that." He walked away, continuing his steps.

Alfred muttered to himself, "That's if I don't kill you."

Roger, as he walked, replied: "Try if you can.

Commander Laurent emerged from his room addressing General Alfred, who was in a state of shock, and said to him, "I'm hosting a lunch today and I hope that... What's wrong with you? What's bothering you!?

Alfred, with fear and confusion, exclaimed:

I swear Roger is possessed!

Laurent responded: "Roger again!!

What's your problem with him!?

Alfred replied: "Don't worry about it, it's my issue, and I'll deal with it my way.

✳✳✳

On July 14, 1789, the French Revolution erupted.

The hungry and destitute rose up from the poor, stormed the Bastille prison, which the public considered a symbol of tyranny. The revolution escalated, and monarchy was on the brink of collapse. The rebels gradually gained control over many areas in Paris. The wavering and weak government responded to the rebels with all cruelty and brutality, but the end was very near, without a doubt.Louis XVI became almost imprisoned in Versailles Palace, or rather, he became like a madman. All his actions became insane, with the rebels, with the general public, and even inside the palace.

✳✳✳

While Catherine was asleep in her room after midnight, she opened her eyes to the sound of the door opening. She saw a group of guards running towards her and dragging her from her bed.

She started screaming, but one of the guards placed his hand over her mouth to silence her, causing her to lose consciousness.

When she opened her eyes, she found herself tied to a bed in a room that seemed to be the king's chamber.

She felt the door opening, and the king entered.

He closed the door behind him and approached her with lecherous looks and a contemptible laugh, saying: "Welcome, my dear Catherine, welcome to my kingdom. You are mine now, and I will do with you as I please. No one will stop me, for François is not here now to defend you.

Catherine tried to scream even though her mouth was covered, so he said to her:

Calm down, my little whore, for no matter how much you scream, no one will hear you. And even if someone hears your scream, they will not dare to save you from my hands.

And he attacked her with all his vulgarity,

Catherine lost consciousness. Her soft body was too weak to endure the king's brutality.

After hours, she opened her eyes and saw an angelic face. It was Queen Marie Antoinette, who began to untie her while exclaiming, "Why are you here?! And why are you tied up in this terrible way?! And who did this to you?!

Catherine, with a trembling voice, replied:

"He's a vile person who you know him well!

Antoinette fell silent for a moment, then said: Catherine, I don't know what to say to you! My husband's behavior puts me in very embarrassing situations..

Catherine interrupted her: "My lady, don't worry about me.. Who am I? I'm just a lost soul in this dirty world. Everyone abandoned me, my family abandoned me, people abandoned me, François abandoned me, even God abandoned me and forgot me..

She began to cry bitterly and said:

"Why did all this happen to me? and what sin did I commit to deserve such harsh punishment? And why was I created and came to this world?.. How much I need my mother's bosom, I miss her so much... I want to return to her bosom, to her warm embrace. I want to regain my innocent face like the face of childhood. I want to leave this dirty world.

Antoinette comforted her and stroked her hair, saying:

"Don't worry, my dear Catherine, for I am with you, and I will remain with you until the last breath of my life, and I will never abandon you, no matter what the circumstances.

Catherine said: "My lady, you must leave this palace, this city, and this country altogether, for your life is in imminent danger, and the angry mobs are approaching the palace, and they will never spare you, and they will seek revenge on you if you fall into their hands. My life doesn't matter to me as much as yours does, my lady..

Isn't your brother the Emperor of Austria? Go to Austria then, for time is running out, and it's only a matter of time before the revolutionaries storm the palace.

Antoinette replied: "Yes, my dear Catherine, I have come to realize this very well. Neither I nor anyone else can fix all the damage caused by Louis XVI and his ancestors.. Then why do these common people want to take revenge on me?! What is my fault if I live in this luxurious palace? And what is my fault if I am the wife of a cowardly, weak, and filthy king like Louis XVI? And do these common people think that I am happy in my life?! No, by heaven, I am not. Do they envy me for the life of luxury that I live?! Let them take it all, for I am tired of this empty life. I have come to read the future very well, for what is to come is much worse than what has passed. And I have come to know my fate very well. Something inside me tells me that my end is very near. And the only thing I have now and will never give up is the will and strength. I want you, too, to be strong so that you won't collapse, my dear Catherine. Oh, if you only knew the darkness of the coming days."

Catherine smiled despite her sadness and said:

"My lady, every day I discover something new in you that increases my admiration for you. In the past, I found innocence, spontaneity, and childhood in you. Now I discover strength of will and a strong iron personality. How can a person embody all these wonderful contradictions? These contradictions have never and will never come together over the ages except in one person, and that person is Marie Antoinette.

Antoinette: "Thank you for your praise, anyway. Let me help you get out of this dirty room, and rest assured that what happened to you today will never happen again. I know how to restrain Louis. Perhaps I can't stop all his savagery at once, but at least I will keep this savagery away from you.

∗∗∗

"After two days, Catherine's room..

A person wearing a long hat and elegant attire enters, carrying a black bag in his right hand and a bunch of papers in his left. He asks for permission to sit and addresses Catherine, saying: you are Lady Catherine, am I not mistaken?

Catherine responds: "No, you are not mistaken, but what do you want?

He replies: "First, let me introduce myself. I am the lawyer Joe Raymond. Countess Julie Anna Debari recommended you as the sole inheritor of her wealth just days before her death. As her lawyer, I have come to complete the procedures of the will and inform you of the matter.

Catherine is surprised by what she hears and asks:

"She recommended her wealth to me? Why me specifically?

The lawyer explains: "At first, I was as surprised as you!

I asked her about the reason for her sudden decision and the timing of this decision. Her response was that you are the only one deserving of this wealth.

She felt she was going to die. That's what I read in her eyes. In any case, she had no heir. She was, as you know, alone without any relatives.

"Thank you anyway," Catherine responds, "You can now dispose of her assets without any constraints.. Now please allow me to leave, the lawyer saysthat, and exits the room.

Catherine didn't care at all about this news, and no trace of joy appeared on her face.

Moments later, Queen Marie Antoinette entered, smiling, saying: "My dear Catherine, you are now rich. You have become noble. Of course, you cannot remain a mere maid while possessing all this wealth!

...What's wrong with you, Catherine?! I don't see signs of joy on your face!!

 Catherine: How can I be happy, my lady? I have lost the dearest people to my heart. I have lost them forever. I lost Francois forever, and I lost the countess forever.

The countess Julie, that woman characterized by qualities not found in angels. Imagine, even though I was her rival, and despite the short time she knew me, she recommended her entire wealth to me!

Throughout my life, I have never seen anyone as faithful and loyal as her, nor with such a big heart.

I have never seen anyone love like her.

But she loved someone who didn't deserve that love..

and so did I...I also loved someone who didn't deserve it. I loved the same person!

Antoinette began to console her and wiped her tears, saying: "Don't worry, dear Catherine. Your tears won't help. Forget the past and its sorrows and start your life anew.

 Catherine: How can I forget, my lady? How can I start any life? Is there even a life now? You know very well that the end is near as the revolutionaries take over the country. We are now besieged, and it won't be long before this palace falls into their hands. And after that, there will be no use for any wealth..

Catherine collapsed onto Antoinette's chest, crying, her tears flowing freely.

Antoinette began to cry too, but she quickly wiped her tears and said: "Be strong, dear Catherine, don't be afraid.

✳ ✳ ✳

"As the months passed, the revolution grew stronger. The army's suppression of the revolution became more violent, Louis XVI became more insane, and Marie Antoinette became increasingly helpless. And Catherine became more miserable and fearful of the inevitable dark fate awaiting her.

After a few days, at the entrance of Versailles Palace...Roger approaches the palace door holding a knife he was playing with in his right hand.

He approaches one of the guards and says to him:

"Hey, you, go and tell the queen that I want to meet her.

The guard responds rudely: "Get out of here immediately. Who are you to dare to request a meeting with the queen!?

Roger pauses for a moment, looks at the guard, then laughs mockingly, saying: "I won't kill you. Do you know why? Because you are new here, and that's why you don't know who you're talking to..

Two guards approached him, and one of them said: "This is you, Roger!! I see you here. If you are looking for trouble, please understand that our troubles are enough for us..

Roger approached, saying: "Oh, the irony. You have developed a tongue, Lilian, and you know how to speak!

Lilian, the guard, asked: "What do you want!?"

Roger: "It's none of your concern..

and continued walking towards the door.

Lilian: "You're not allowed to enter."

Roger: "Stop me if you can," he said, continuing his steps inside.

One of the guards said to Lilian: "Why not shoot him? Are you going to let him enter!?"

Lilian: "I am not ready to sacrifice my life for such foolishness. And even if I shoot him and miss, do you know what will happen to me? I'll be dead for sure.

Then you do it and show us your bravery."

After a moment of silence, the guard said: "I will."

Moments later, Roger found himself surrounded by more than twenty guards with guns..

One of the guards approached him, saying: "You will enter the palace as you wish, but not to meet the queen, but to enter the prison.

A voice from behind the guards said: "Leave him alone, step away from him. I'll take care of him..

The guards stepped back, and Lilian addressed Roger:

"I will accompany you to the queen, but promise me to be calm and not cause trouble..

Roger smiled: "I'll try, but I can't promise," as they began to walk inside the palace..

While walking, Roger collided with someone, causing papers

to fall from that person's hand..

Roger yelled at him: "Are you blind? Can't you see in front of you!"

The person apologized and left, and Roger turned to Lilian, asking: "Who is this young man!? What a polite person. Did you see how he apologized to me!?"

Lilian explained: "He is Colonel Napoleon, the son of Carlo Charles Bonaparte, a nobleman from Corsica. He studied at the king's expense and is now one of the smartest and most skilled artillery officers. I think he was meeting the king."

Roger, smiling: "You know! some time ago, someone bumped into me in the same way, and he didn't survive thereafter. But I didn't kill him, I don't know why! I feel like this young man will have a great future..

Lilian agreed: "You're right. Everyone who meets him feels this way, even though he's not yet twenty.

Roger changed the subject: "Anyway, let's forget about him.. I wanted to ask you.. I always knew you were a scoundrel! so where did you get the ethics to behave as you did?"

Roger explained: "I wanted to repay your kindness.. You did me a favor in the past, which I will never forget throughout my life..

Lilian: "So, it's a matter of returning the favor!! But what favor are you talking about!?"

Roger: "Don't you remember? You helped my mother when she was sick with the plague, and you paid for her treatment from your own money..

What is the value of what I do with you today compared to your saving my mother's life? No matter what you do, I will not return to you even a small part of what you gave."

Roger: Oh, I remembered.. Never mind, I do things that may be good or they may be bad.. but I forget them immediately and do not stop at them..

Lillian: If you forgot, I have not and will not forget.

.. After a moment, they reached the queen's room.

Lilian entered the room after saluting, and Antoinette was sitting on her rocking chair with a golden fan in her hand.

Lilian informed: "Your Majesty, there is someone who wants to meet you.

Antoinette: "Someone wants to meet me! Who is it!?"

Lilian: "It's Roger..

Antoinette, with fear and confusion: "You said who, what does he want?"

Lilian: "As you command, Your Majesty..

Roger entered the room without permission and bowed

before the queen.

Lilian, emotionally: "We didn't agree on this, Roger!

Roger replied: "We didn't agree on anything. You might have agreed with yourself..

Antoinette, addressing Lilian: "You can leave now, but leave the door open and make sure you are with the guards nearby."

Lilian left the room.

Antoinette to Roger, who was silent: "Why aren't you speaking? Say what you want!

Roger: "I didn't come to talk, but to see your angelic face and admire it. I've missed you so much..

Antoinette, with fear and agitation: "If you have any intentions, I warn you..

Roger interrupted: "I have no intentions to harm you. Even if I had such intentions, I would have done so when we met some time ago. I think you remember, as the opportunity was more favorable then, surrounded by all the guards and soldiers filling the palace. Despite that, if I wanted to do something, I wouldn't fear them all..

Antoinette acknowledged: "You saved my life, and I am grateful to you now. So, ask what you want, and you shall be granted, except for one request that you know is out of reach..

Roger assured: "Don't worry, I won't ask for that request, even though I desire it with all my heart.. In fact, I won't ask for anything. I don't expect anything in return for any service I provide.

"But I came to protect you and be your personal guard, especially since François left the palace. That's what I want.

Antoinette agreed: "You have it."

Roger thanked her: "Thank you, Your Majesty, for this honor you have bestowed upon me. I promise to be loyal to you until the end of my days.

Antoinette asked: "Will you abandon that cursed revolution you joined?

Roger replied: "Forgive me, Your Majesty, whether I leave that revolution you call cursed or not is my own affair. What matters is that I will fulfill my duty in protecting you to the best of my ability. You are the important one to me. Let the king and the revolutionaries go to hell. I'll be with the revolution, but if this revolution comes close to you, I'll crush it over the heads of its people.

 And now, allow me to leave.

Catherine's room..

Roger opens the door and enters.

Catherine, fearfully: Who are you, and what do you want?

Roger, after finding a place to sit:

You can trust me.

Catherine: If you intend harm, I warn you. I am the queen's maid...and..

Roger interrupts: I said you can trust me. Firstly, let me introduce myself. I am Roger Dubier, the new personal guard for the queen. I know your story with Francois; he's my friend and hides nothing from me. I'm here to protect you, so trust me.

Catherine: Did Francois send you?

Roger: Whether he did or not is irrelevant. No one can dictate to me. But Francois's head is wanted now, as you know. I'm here to protect you on his behalf.

Catherine, speaking to herself softly:

He still loves me! ..She pauses, then continues:

Anyway, I'll pay you for this protection.

Roger laughs incredulously: Pay me? You!

Catherine: It's a long story. I'm wealthy now. Countess Julie

Anne de Barry left me her entire fortune.

Roger chuckles again: She left her fortune to you? That's strange! Anyway, I don't need money. Keep your wealth. It might help you in dark times ahead. And if you still doubt my intentions, know this well: it's not Roger who betrays his friends.

Then straightens up and walks away.

✳✳✳

A bar in a suburb of Paris.

Two men sit drinking, their faces showing signs of intoxication.

One of them, laughing: You know, this revolution only lacked Francois! the son of a whore, to join it.

The other: You're right. My father used to visit his mother... What was her name? Oh yes, Theodora.

The first one laughs mockingly: Maybe... Francois was your father's son or mine. Don't rule anything out.

The bar owner, laughing: Yes, his mother was foolish, but I loved her despite her stupidity.

He laughs loudly, and everyone in the bar joins in... Suddenly, his voice chokes, and his laughter fades under the grip of a strong arm around his neck. It's Roger, who has caught both men in his left arm, while his right arm wraps around the bar owner's neck.

He begins: You scoundrels.. If you were men, you'd say this to Francois's face. But you're cowards.

Then, he turns to the bar owner, who is choking between his hands, saying: If these fools had said that, I would have just killed them and smashed some chairs and tables. But since it was you, it means the whole bar will be punished...

He looks at the people sitting:

You heard what was said "and laughed foolishly".. All of you will die today.

He turns back to the bar owner: You'll be the last.

and throws him onto the bottles lined up on the table.

The owner falls unconscious, his body covered in blood. Then, Roger grabs both men by their collars, laughing, saying: I'll try something I haven't done to anyone in a long time. then smashes their heads together.. and they fall to the ground with shattered skulls. Then, he steps on them as he walks past the trembling customers, who are terrified by what they witnessed..

He approaches them, saying:

You will die today. There's no debate about it. But there are some rules to this collective death..

Firstly, let all the women leave the bar. I don't like killing women. I'll spare them for other purposes after I'm done here. Secondly, and he laughs, oh, there's no second..

I'll leave now,, I have many things to do.

He turns to leave, and as he reaches the door, he turns back to them, saying: I forgot to tell you something..

Last night, I stole some explosives from the army..

Theft isn't my habit because thieves are bad, and I'm not a bad man.. But now that it's happened, I planted these explosives at every corner of this place while listening to the conversation between these two fools I just killed.

This place will be destroyed in moments. My advice to you is this: anyone who tries to leave will die a gruesome death at my hands outside. So, I suggest you choose death by explosion. It's better for you..

And now, I'll go. See you in hell.

He laughs and leaves.

Moments later, a loud explosion shakes the entire neighborhood.

Roger leans against a tree nearby, saying: That's the fate of those who mess with my friends.

He laughs heartily and leaves the scene.

***

Commander Laurent's room.

He stands up, hits the table with his hand, and says:

Who does Roger think he is? Instead of killing the king's soldiers, he kills the revolutionaries!

Alfred: You're right, he has indeed crossed the line too far.

Laurent angrily: I'll summon him here and punish him severely..

Roger enters after throwing one of the people standing at the door to the ground, approaching Laurent, saying:

Here I am before you, punish me, what are you waiting for!

Laurent, shouting: You've gone too far, today you burned down a tavern and killed over thirty people, and tomorrow, God knows what you'll do!

Roger falls silent for a moment, then says:

I promise you that you'll soon be relieved of my presence, he says, staring at Alfred, who was trembling with fear and signs of terror on his face..

He continues his speech: You'll be rid of me, but not before I fulfill an old covenant I made.

He begins to approach Alfred, saying:

You've scattered my family and taken over the small house they lived in. I emigrated with my family to America to start a new life.. but you destroyed my life!

My entire family died of hunger and cold because of you..

Alfred, fearfully: Understand me, Roger, it wasn't in my hands. I was ordered to take over the house to turn the place into a military barracks for the British army. Believe me, it wasn't in my hands. Please believe me, in the name of the friendship that once united us..

Roger, mockingly: Friendship, you say! A friendship between an occupying commander and a revolutionary! Believe me, you who thought you were my friend, logic rejects such a relationship between the oppressor and the oppressed laborer.. Then he looks at Laurent, who was shocked, and says to him:

Listen to what this dirty Englishman is saying!!

He is my friend and he takes advantage of my absence to scatter my family and commit the worst atrocities against them! Then he turns back and looks at Alfred, saying:

I will never forget in my life the scene of my family whom you threw into the cold and nakedness. I will never forget that scene as they scattered in the snows of harsh American winters. I vowed to myself to kill you in the most heinous way imaginable, and the time has come to fulfill this promise.

He turns to Laurent, saying: You will witness this revenge, and I advise you not to intervene lest you face a fate similar to his..

He begins to approach Alfred, who begins to cry and plead, begging him not to kill him: "I'll give you whatever money you want, I don't want to die."

Roger puts his fist on Alfred's head and says:

This is a method of killing I haven't tried yet. How lucky you are. You will be the first to die by my hand in this way.

In an instant, with his strong hands, he crushes his neck until his head is facing backwards towards his back and hangs backwards.. Then he throws his body on the ground and stomps on it, in full view of Commander Laurent, who could not bear the horror of this scene, so he began vomiting and it looked as if he was about to faint..

Roger looks at him and says: Now that I have finished my revenge, you will finally be relieved of me. You won't see my face anymore, or who knows!! We may meet under better circumstances..

He finishes his words and leaves.

***

One of the poor streets of Paris..

François was sitting at one of the entrances of the old houses, cleaning his rifle.

Roger comes and sits beside him.

François: So, you've become Antoinette's personal guard!

Roger: Yes, that's true. I have to protect her. Then he laughs and says: Look at the irony of fate! Your head has become wanted in the palace, and now I have become wanted by the leaders of the revolution!

François: So, we have to switch roles.

Roger stands up and says: Yes, my friend, that's what has already happened. And now, I have to go. The queen needs someone to protect her, especially in these difficult circumstances..

François stands up and says: Roger, I entrust you with Catherine. She's alone now.

Roger: Don't worry, my friend, I will never let you down as long as I live.

***

On October 5th, 1789, the revolutionaries began to march towards the Palace of Versailles, and they began to destroy everything they saw in front of them. Queen Antoinette was forced to move with her husband Louis XVI to the Tuileries Palace in Paris, where they were almost confined.

✱✱✱

Tuileries Palace, Queen's Chamber..

Roger enters the queen's chamber, with bloodstains on his face and clothes.

Antoinette to Roger: What's wrong? What is this blood on your clothes?

Roger, smiling: They were a group of soldiers in the palace whom I heard speaking ill of you, so I killed them. That's the story in a nutshell.

Antoinette was lost in thought, sad.

Roger: What's wrong, my lady? What's the secret of this sadness on your beautiful face?

Antoinette: What occupies my mind is Catherine! She disappeared since that fateful day, the day of the fall of the Palace of Versailles, and I don't know her fate or anything about her.

And she started crying, saying: Do you think she's alive or

dead?

Roger, gently passing his hand over Antoinette's head and caressing her blonde hair: Trust me completely, my lady, that I will spare no effort in searching for her if she's alive.

I will do it for you, my lady, and for my lifelong friend François, who entrusted her to me. I tried to save her that day. But she disappeared. I tried to search for her but found no trace of her! and this torments me, for I feel that I failed François and was not up to the responsibility..

After wiping her tears, Antoinette says: You, Roger, did everything you could, so don't blame yourself beyond your capacity.

Then she says to me that you were protecting her for François's sake!! Where is this François! He left and left everything behind after killing the woman he loved and left Catherine to her black fate.

Roger: François has faced and continues to face pressures that mountains cannot bear. This world has taken everything from him. He lost his family and his dignity. He lost everyone he loved, and these reasons are enough to make a person lose his sanity. In addition to the fact that Catherine always refused to return to him, whenever I broached the subject, she violently refused, and this only added to François's suffering.

Antoinette: But Catherine still loved him. I could see that in her eyes..

Roger: Anyway, François changed a lot after leaving the Palace of Versailles. He was always calm and balanced, but he became nervous and emotional. His first and last goal now is revenge..

Antoinette: Is he perhaps seeking revenge from me!?

Roger: I don't know exactly, but I don't think so.. And even if he wanted to, he won't be able to as long as I am here. But I believe he loves you and won't hurt you. Whenever I talk about you in front of him, he enters a state of sadness and silence, then changes the subject. This is always his condition whenever he hears your name.

✳✳✳

One of the palace corridors in the evening..

Roger was with Lillian.

Lillian: How I hate that despicable king..

Roger: I share the same feeling, and my hatred for him grows day by day. How I wish I could gouge out his eyes.

Lillian: I hate the queen too..

Roger looks at her sharply and angrily.

Lillian, confused and scared: Oh, what a fool I am! I forgot who I was speaking in front of.. I didn't mean...

Roger: I advise you not to forget again and not to speak about Antoinette in this manner, not in front of me or anyone else. For nothing, just to avoid being killed..

✳✳✳

Night of June 21, 1791, the king's chamber..

Louis XVI addresses Antoinette.

King: Won't your cursed brother send us support? Your brother Leopold II, who calls himself the Holy Roman Emperor! Damn him and his sanctity.. We requested assistance two years ago. What is he waiting for?

Antoinette, angrily: Stop talking about my brother like this.

He offered me to go to him in Austria. He won't involve his armies in a battle with the revolutionaries..

Roger enters addressing the queen: All arrangements are ready, and tonight is very suitable for departure..

The king addresses him angrily: When I'm present, you address me! I am the king..

Roger ignores his words and continues addressing Antoinette: You will disguise as commoners, and at the palace gate, you will find a carriage to take you to Austria. I will accompany you to ensure your protection. Prepare yourself, my lady, for the road ahead is long and full of dangers.

The king shouts: I will not leave France. I am its king, and I will remain its king..

He walks away shouting, leaving the room..

Roger addressing Antoinette: If he doesn't leave with you, leave him to his fate.. Perhaps he will fall into the hands of the revolutionaries and get what he deserves..

Antoinette: He will come with me.. I will convince him.

Roger gets agitated: What forces you to do that? And why are you so insistent on taking that despicable man with you?

Antoinette: I don't want future generations to say that I abandoned my husband at such a crucial moment.. That's why I insist.

Antoinette disguised as ordinary travelers along with Louis XVI as well. They succeeded in leaving Paris, heading to Austria.

$$*\,*\,*$$

Region of Varennes, southeast of Paris..

They arrived in the carriage that was taking them there.

One of the nearby people says to another:

Look at that carriage! The queen Antoinette is inside it..

The other says: Yes, it's her. Let's gather men to capture her and hand her over to the revolution leaders.

Minutes later, gunshots rang out, and hundreds of people rushed, surrounding the carriage from all sides.

Louis XVI seemed trembling in one corner of the carriage, while Antoinette bravely got out of the carriage to face the crowds, followed by Roger.

As she got out, someone aimed a shot at her, which Roger intercepted in his shoulder while defending her.

He threw a knife, piercing the head of the person who fired, and carried Antoinette in his arms, kissing her on the forehead, saying:

"This is the day I've longed for. This is the death I wished for and deserve, for you."

He kissed her lips and put her back in the carriage, closing the door..

Then he turned to the crowds, saying:

"The time for play has come, you scoundrels."

Then he shouted:

Who among you wants to harm the queen must first step over my body..

He began to approach the crowds steadily, his eyes ablaze.

Some began to retreat under the influence of his gaze, while others started aiming their guns at him..

Roger kept advancing, and bullets started raining on him from all directions. He drew his sword from its sheath and began swinging it right and left..

Heads began to fall by the dozens until the ground was littered with them..

Roger fell to the ground after receiving more than fifty bullets in his body, and he breathed his last, saying:

"I offer you my death, my beloved Antoinette, for you."

And he closed his eyes, departing life.

Antoinette and Louis XVI were captured and brought back to Paris as prisoners, where they were presented to the Revolutionary Court on charges of high treason.

The attempt to escape only fueled people's hatred towards them.

The king was executed by guillotine on January 21, 1793.

As for Antoinette, she remained imprisoned indefinitely.

The delay in issuing her execution sentence was attributed to two reasons, according to some neutral historians.

Most of those who wrote about that period belonged to a group of writers who were fervent supporters of the revolution and harbored resentment towards the monarchy.

The first reason for the delay in issuing the execution sentence, according to those neutral historians, was the revolution leaders' fear of the wrath of her brother, the Emperor of Austria.

After the revolutionaries invaded Tuileries Palace and arrested Antoinette and Louis XVI, Leopold II, the Emperor of Austria, formed an alliance with the King of Prussia and threatened military intervention and the occupation of France to free Antoinette from captivity.

The second reason was attributed to the strong attachment of a section of the French people to their queen..

They hadn't forgotten their great love for her since her arrival in France. She was a wonderful dream for every French citizen, both commoners and nobles. They always anticipated her appearance from her balcony to address the people, and they always cheered her name.

But fate was stronger than this love.

What Louis XVI and his predecessors sowed, Marie Antoinette reaped.. The extremists among the common people and the leaders of the revolution, who exerted great pressure on the court, issued the death sentence.

✳✳✳

Queen's Prison..

Antoinette sits in a corner, her hands resting on her face, showing signs of exhaustion and fatigue, her blonde hair falling forward.

Francois enters, kisses her on the head, and sits on the ground next to her without speaking. After a period of silence, he turns to her and says:

"Please, my lady, don't torture me further. Your silence is killing me.. I suffer from being unable to do anything. You haven't spoken to me for days. Please, show me one way to bring a smile back to your face.

A group of soldiers enters and grabs Antoinette to take her out of prison. One of the soldiers turns to Francois and says, "Come on, get yourself ready to come with us. In a few hours, the execution ceremonies will begin."

Francois, raising his head to the sky, tears starting to fill his eyes: "Oh God, what do I do? Tell me what to do.. Guide me, for I am lost, I am falling apart. Help me, oh God."

He falls to his knees, tears filling his face.

October 16, 1793,

On that sad autumn morning..

Catherine sleeps on one of the corners of the poor streets of Paris, with her three-year-old daughter next to her. Three years have passed since the fall of Versailles Palace. Catherine survived by sheer luck that bloody day.

Her situation since that fateful day has been dire, regardless of it being one of the happiest days for the poor French people. She didn't want much from this world, just a safe place to sleep and the embrace of a loved one she had been abandoned by. She loved with innocent, pure affection, but they tainted her serene fountain and sowed thorns in her path. This is how she ended up, sleeping on the edges of roads, eating whatever she could find, her body violated by every passerby, with no one to protect her, no family, no law. Chaos still ravaged the country like fire consumes dry wood.

Catherine opens her eyes to the sound of heavy footsteps in

one of the nearby streets. She sees a massive procession advancing, with a carriage resembling a cage at its center. Inside that cage is a woman of exquisite beauty. Catherine's eyes widen to take in what she sees before her. It's Queen Marie Antoinette, bound in iron and wearing her royal gown, torn at the edges from prison. The procession slowly passes by, and towards the end, a group of soldiers, led by a man with a long beard and long hair, marches. Despite his hair covering most of his face, Catherine finds this man familiar.

One of them shouts: "Hurry up, Francois, we must arrive before noon. The execution ceremonies will begin then." Catherine dispels any doubt and, before she can even think, runs towards Francois, calling his name. The soldiers try to hold her back, but she continues to scream and cry out: "Francois, it's me, Catherine. Have you forgotten me? If you can hear me, just look at me.

" When her resistance increases, one of the soldiers strikes her with his rifle, knocking her to the ground.

Blood starts to flow from her face, and in that moment, Francois turns to look at her, his face filled with both cruelty and sorrow. Then he continued on his way."

Minutes later, Catherine regained some of her consciousness.

She carried her baby girl and began crawling on the ground,

her blood leaving traces everywhere she passed...until she reached the place where the death sentence was being carried out. Crowds of people were gathered in a large square, and in the middle of that square was a huge guillotine and a number of soldiers leading Queen Marie Antoinette until they stopped her In front of that guillotine.

Someone says to her: We will now execute the death sentence on you. Is there a word you would like to say at this moment before the sentence is carried out?

Antoinette smiles confidently and says:

My words will not be for you, but will be for the masses... She moves forward with firm and confident steps, stands addressing those huge crowds:

O French people, you have carried out the revolution. Congratulations to you for it. Today you declare your victory! May everyone be happy with his victory..

If you think that you have defeated me, you are wrong.

And if you think that you will see my weakness today, you are also wrong..

O people, know well:

And remember these words of mine, and let history remember them..

The courage that I have shown throughout my life and

throughout the past years, Do you think that I will abandon this courage at this moment? when all my suffering will end! No, for the sake of heaven, I will never abandon it.

These were her last words.

Catherine could not believe what her eyes were seeing. She started crying..

She felt Antoinette's gaze, which she caught sight of among those crowds.

She felt her eyes saying to her as before:

"Do not be afraid, dear Catherine, I am with you"

The soldiers placed Antoinette's head in the guillotine, beginning her execution ceremony.

Catherine looked around and found François standing in a place not very far from the place where the death sentence was being carried out, surrounded by a group of soldiers. Catherine stood on her feet despite her extreme fatigue and carried her baby girl, and she came to her with strength that only God knows.

she runs towards François and grabbed him by his military shirt. She began to kiss his hands, begging him:

François, please, do something for the queen.

Please.. I will kiss your hands, I will even kiss your feet.

Save her and let them kill me instead..

François turned to her without speaking, with signs of sadness evident on his face.

Catherine looked at him with sad, depressing, miserable, desperate looks..

Looks with a thousand question marks!

After a few moments of silence under the influence of her gaze, Francois tells the guards in a desperate voice:

"Get her out of here immediately."

The guards rush towards her, dragging her away as she continues to scream and cry out:

"What has happened to you, Francois? How did your heart become so cruel? I am not the one who killed your family, nor is the queen! Tell me who you seek revenge on! I loved you, Francois, and I still do, and I will love you forever." The soldiers pull her away, her screams fading bit by bit. Francois pays no attention to her screams or her words, he is oblivious to everything around him.

Commander Laurent stands next to Francois..

Laurent addressing François: "What a historic day! The Queen of France is being led to her death.

Do you know, François, I pity her, especially after her

brother's army was defeated at the Battle of Valmy and all hope of saving her life vanished.. No one can save her now.. her fate is sealed without a doubt.

François turns to Laurent and says sadly: "I can't do anything." He repeats it angrily, "I can't do anything, and that's what torments me."

Laurent continues: "Do you think I'm unaware?

You visited her secretly in her prison, conveyed messages to her brother! and participated in two failed attempts to rescue her from captivity.. Don't deny it!

I know everything.

François turns to him, smiling with a desperate smile, then turns away.

Laurent continues, "Do you know why I turned a blind eye to all your betrayals? Because I pity you. You and this arrogant queen deserve pity..

François angrily: "Pity yourself first!" and punches Laurent, knocking him to the ground, his face bleeding.

and stands over him and says: "My friend Roger was very merciful not to kill you outright! He had a little pity! But as for me, life has taken everything from me.. I don't even have that little bit left..

He picks up a big rock and throws it at Laurent's head, then lifts the rock from his own head, which looks shattered and stuck to the ground..

He throws the rock towards some crowds, saying to them, "Make way, you scoundrels!" and rides his horse through the crowds, piercing them.

The guillotine falls on Antoinette's head, and she passes away. Her head rolls on the ground.

When the people saw this scene, they all fell silent. The crowd that had been cheering for the queen's death moments ago now felt the weight of what had happened. They realized they hadn't killed the queen; they had killed themselves..

In another corner of the square, Catherine lay on the ground clutching her young daughter, while three soldiers beat her mercilessly, leaving her almost unconscious. Suddenly, a bullet pierces the heart of one of the soldiers beating her, followed by another bullet hitting another soldier's head. The third soldier retreats in fear..

François approaches him, saying: "You fools! I told you to just move her, not beat her like savages."

The soldier responds fearfully: This is treason! What you did is treason, and I will report it to the revolution leaders to deal with you and punish you for your actions..

François smiles: "That's if you stay alive."!

He draws his sword and swiftly decapitates the soldier, then smirks and looks at the severed head, saying:

"Now go and tell whoever you want."

He continues, "Damn you and this cursed revolution. "Thugs revolting against thugs.”

 Antoinette's head won't be the only one severed in this revolution, I swear it..

Then he turns to Catherine, lying on the ground in a pitiful state. He approaches her, kisses her forehead, and whispers in her ear: "Catherine, go back to your village. It's the safest place for you, my beloved Catherine. I won't swear by my military honor; that honor is a shame I'll carry for life.. But I swear by Antoinette's spirit that I will return to you one day, and I won't break that promise..

But for now, I must go. I have some scores to settle."

And François leaves, leaving Catherine behind.

Perhaps he should have stayed with her..

perhaps it was his duty to take her back to her village and stay by her side..

for he still loves her deeply, unchanged by the years..

However, vengeance blinded his heart. Vengeance against

everything, against those who killed his mother and brothers, against those who killed Antoinette, against those who killed his lifelong friend Roger..

His hatred was for the whole world, or perhaps he wanted to avenge himself because he killed Julie with his own hands. Little did he know that he would lose Catherine forever.

Catherine was unaware of what was happening, but every word François uttered was engraved in her memory. His promise to return became an obsession in her life.

The revolution ended, years passed, and here is Catherine returning to her village, where childhood memories reside, returning to forget. Perhaps that small cottage where she grew up will help her forget the years of misery.

Perhaps distancing herself from people will help her forget.

Every day, she sits by that bleak window, hoping to see him emerge from the fog, hoping he will come with the procession of Queen Antoinette, hoping he will save her again and carry her in his arms to the Palace of Versailles.

She is ready now to forget everything he did to her, to forget all her suffering when she sees him emerge from the mist.

She waits longingly, nothing but fog, nothing but sad

memories haunting her.

Nothing but the frost engulfing her body and heart, and her daughter, who hasn't even reached the age of ten, sitting trembling from the cold and sorrow in a corner of that cottage.

They stole her childhood from her face, walking the path of her mother's sorrow as if fate had decreed the same harsh judgment on both mother and daughter.

Catherine looks at her daughter with deep sorrow, as if reading her future, helpless to save that innocent girl from her inevitable fate.

Days pass, and that day Catherine had long awaited finally arrives. The little girl was gathering some firewood beside the house when she sees a man with a long beard and long hair through the fog.

He approaches the girl and calls out, "Little girl, is this Catherine's house?"

She answers fearfully, "Yes, it's my mother's.

Who are you?"

When she hears his words, he runs towards her, picks her up, and embraces her. "I'm your father. I've come back."

She shouts with joy:

I'll go tell my mother. She's sitting by the window as usual. I think she's seen you now..

The girl runs to the cottage to tell her mother the news she has waited for for years..

She enters and calls out, "Mother, Father has returned. Wake up, Mother, he's back..

François enters, his daughter turns to him, trembling:

She won't wake up. Please, Father, wake her up!

When François hears these words, he runs to Catherine and weeps bitterly on her chest:

"Not now, Catherine, please don't leave me now. I've come as I promised you. Forgive me, I know I don't deserve it, and I don't deserve a wonderful woman like you, my rose, my star, my crown.

My first and last love, I have wronged you greatly, my sweetheart, I have wronged everyone. I have wronged you and everyone who loved me..

He pauses for a moment, his tears turning into blood, then continues sadly:

I saw Antoinette being slaughtered before my eyes and said nothing! I saw her being led to the guillotine and didn't burn all of France! I saw her innocent head rolling before me and didn't turn the world upside down over those who executed her! Oh, and I killed Julie with my own hands.. And now I see you dying before me!

He falls silent for a moment, his tone filled with anger towards himself:

"It is I who killed you long ago. I don't deserve to live."

He kept repeating these words, crying on Catherine's chest for hours.

In that moment, he wishes he could turn back time to change something, but it's futile. Everything has ended, leaving only memories. These memories haunted him for years, memories too heavy to bear.

Our memories always outweigh us, whether they are happy or sad!

Can one death end all these memories?

Or perhaps, death is the best remedy..

The next morning, the villagers gather upon hearing the little girl's cries, only to find François dead on Catherine's chest. He died with his hand holding hers. One of the onlookers, tears filling his eyes, says, "Poor girl, she waited for him for so long, only for him to return too late." Another remarks:

He dreamt of returning to her embrace, and now he stays with her forever..

....

Grief completes its cycle, and a new chapter of sorrow begins with the little girl, now orphaned and alone.

She leaves her village to follow in her mother's footsteps, and thus ends the story of one death, only for another to begin.

- The End -

Don't miss out!
Visit the website below and you can sign up to receive emails whenever khalil altahhan publishes a new obligation.

BOOKS2READ

https://books2read.com/r/B-A-EYQBB-PAZXC

Connecting independent readers to independent writers.

About the Author

Khalil Altahhan is a Syrian author. He was born in Damascus in 1984 and studied law at Damascus University before he was forced to emigrate due to the war. He writes novels and poetry, and expresses his feelings, experiences, and hopes through his words. He has two published novels, "The Prophecy of the Eternal Winter" and "Tears of Angels," and two books of poetry, "Before You Shed My Blood" and "Diary of a Damascene Wound." He is also working on finishing several other novels. His writing is inspired by the harsh conditions of life, war, asylum, and grief. He is a writer who graduated from the school of sadness and harsh life, and seeks to spread peace, love, and hope through his works. You can contact him via email: khalil4love@hotmail.com
Or follow his page on YouTube:
youtube.com/@lover4damascus